S.S.F. Public Library
West Orange
840 West Orange Ave.
South San Francisco, CA 94080

OCT 2005

Hispanic Heritage

Title List

Central American Immigrants to the United States: Refugees from Unrest

Cuban Americans: Exiles from an Island Home

First Encounters Between Spain and the Americas: Two Worlds Meet

Latino Americans and Immigration Laws: Crossing the Border

Latino Americans in Sports, Film, Music, and Government: Trailblazers

Latino Arts and Their Influence on the United States: Songs, Dreams, and Dances

Latino Cuisine and Its Influence on American Foods: The Taste of Celebration

Latino Economics in the United States: Job Diversity

Latino Folklore and Culture: Stories of Family, Traditions of Pride

Latino Migrant Workers: America's Harvesters

Latinos Today: Facts and Figures

The Latino Religious Experience: People of Faith and Vision

Mexican Americans' Role in the United States: A History of Pride, A Future of Hope

Puerto Ricans' History and Promise: Americans Who Cannot Vote

South America's Immigrants to the United States: The Flight from Turmoil

The Story of Latino Civil Rights: Fighting for Justice

S.S.F. PUBLIC LIBRARY
MAIN

Mexican Americans' Role in the United States

A History of Pride, A Future of Hope

by Ellyn Sanna

Mason Crest Publishers
Philadelphia

Mason Crest Publishers Inc.
370 Reed Road
Broomall, Pennsylvania 19008
(866) MCP-BOOK (toll free)

Copyright © 2006 by Mason Crest Publishers. All rights reserved. No part of this publication may be reproduced or transmitted in any form or by any means, electronic or mechanical, including photocopying, recording, taping, or any information storage and retrieval system, without permission from the publisher.

Library of Congress Cataloging-in-Publication Data

Sanna, Ellyn, 1958-
Mexican Americans' role in the United States : a history of pride, a future of hope / by Ellyn Sanna.
p. cm. -- (Hispanic heritage)
Includes index.
Audience: Grades 9-12.
ISBN 1-59084-926-4 ISBN 1-59084-924-8 (series)
1. Mexican Americans--History--Juvenile literature. 2. Mexican Americans--Social conditions--Juvenile literature. 3. Mexico--History--Juvenile literature. I. Title. II. Hispanic heritage (Philadelphia, Pa.)
E184.M5S258 2005
973'.046872073--dc22

2004025796

Interior design by Dianne Hodack.
Produced by Harding House Publishing Service, Inc., Vestal, NY.
Cover design by Dianne Hodack.
Printed and bound in the Hashemite Kingdom of Jordan.

Contents

ONE WAY
MEXICO
OPEN
EN
NEW YORK

Introduction

by José E. Limón, Ph.D.

Even before there was a United States, Hispanics were present in what would become this country. Beginning in the sixteenth century, Spanish explorers traversed North America, and their explorations encouraged settlement as early as the sixteenth century in what is now northern New Mexico and Florida, and as late as the mid-eighteenth century in what is now southern Texas and California.

Later, in the nineteenth century, following Spain's gradual withdrawal from the New World, Mexico in particular established its own distinctive presence in what is now the southwestern part of the United States, a presence reinforced in the first half of the twentieth century by substantial immigration from that country. At the close of the nineteenth century, the U.S. war with Spain brought Cuba and Puerto Rico into an interactive relationship with the United States, the latter in a special political and economic affiliation with the United States even as American power influenced the course of almost every other Latin American country.

The books in this series remind us of these historical origins, even as each explores the present reality of different Hispanic groups. Some of these books explore the contemporary social origins—what social scientists call the "push" factors—behind the accelerating Hispanic immigration to America: political instability, economic underdevelopment and crisis, environmental degradation, impoverished or wholly absent educational systems, and other circumstances contribute to many Latin Americans deciding they will be better off in the United States.

And, for the most part, they will be. The vast majority come to work and work very hard, in order to earn better wages than they would back home. They fill significant labor needs in the U.S. economy and contribute to the economy through lower consumer prices and sales taxes.

When they leave their home countries, many immigrants may initially fear that they are leaving behind vital and important aspects of their home cultures: the Spanish language, kinship ties, food, music, folklore, and the arts. But as these books also make clear, culture is a fluid thing, and these native cultures are not only brought to America, they are also replenished in the United States in fascinating and novel ways. These books further suggest to us that Hispanic groups enhance American culture as a whole.

Our country—especially the young, future leaders who will read these books—can only benefit by the fair and full knowledge these authors provide about the socio-historical origins and contemporary cultural manifestations of America's Hispanic heritage.

1

Mexican Americans

For as long as he can remember, George Elizondo has answered to two names. His friends and teachers call him George, and lately, since he's gotten older, that's what his parents call him, at least most of the time. But sometimes his mother and father forget and call him Jorge (pronounced "hore-hay"), and that's the name his grandparents and aunts and uncles always use. That's what Mrs. Rivera, his mom's best friend, calls him, too, and so do a lot of the people at church. George answers automatically to Jorge—but he thinks of himself as George.

Artwork

Each chapter in this book opens with illustrations designed to resemble yarn paintings, a form of Mexican folk art.

Many Mexican Americans live in New Mexico where their families have lived for centuries.

His parents and grandparents speak Spanish to each other, and George can understand them pretty well when they do—but he's not so good at speaking Spanish himself. As far as he's concerned, English is his native language. He's taking Spanish in school, though, partly because it's easier for him than French, and partly because he knows it will make his grandparents happy if he can talk to them in their language.

The Elizondos live in Rochester, New York, but his mother's family has lived in New Mexico, near Santa Fe, for as long as anyone can remember. His great-great-great-grandfather owned a farm there, and today his Grandma and Grandpa Mendoza still live on the same land. His other grandparents, his father's parents, moved to California from Mexico right after they married. They eventually became American citizens, and all their children were born in the United States. George's parents met in college, and they moved to New York State when George was a baby. Most summers, the Elizondos travel west to visit their family. When George is in California and New Mexico, it seems like almost everyone calls him Jorge.

Sometimes, his Grandma Elizondo tells him stories about Mexico and what it was like to grow up there seventy years ago, but George doesn't feel particularly connected to the land across the border, any more than his friend Joe O'Keefe feels connected to Ireland when his grandmother tells him about the land where she grew up. Lots of people have immigrant grandparents. But Grandpa Mendoza's family has lived in the same place longer than anyone else George knows.

George thinks of himself as a plain old American, rather than a Mexican American. As he grows older, though, he's started to appreciate his Mexican heritage more. He loves the food, the stories, and even the old songs his grandmother sings. "Being Mexican makes us strong," his grandfather told him once. "We aren't like anyone else."

George isn't sure he agrees; he thinks he's pretty much like most everyone else he knows. But still, he's proud of the people who went before him: Grandpa Mendoza's family who has lived on their land for hundreds of years, and Grandma Elizondo's family who were brave enough to start a new life in another country.

Lupe Ortega grew up in Mexico City, where her mother sold fruit on the sidewalks and her father sold gum and candy bars. Lupe remembers when she was very young sitting with her little sister beside her mother's cart. Sometimes people would think she and Pepita were cute, so they would stop to buy a piece of mango or pineapple, or even give the little girls money for nothing. When Lupe got older, her job was to watch for the teenagers on their way to and from school. If the big kids snatched candy without paying, Lupe's mother lost all her profits for the day.

When Lupe's family lived in Mexico, their home was a single room in an old crumbling building built around a central courtyard. One side of the building collapsed during the big earthquake that hit Mexico City back in 1985, before Lupe was born—but the side where the Ortegas lived was still fairly sturdy, even though it was damp, dark, and cramped. Home in those days was a noisy place where you could never be alone. Lots of other kids lived in the building too, though, so she and Pepita always had someone to play with.

But they never had very much to eat, and they didn't see their mother and father much unless they went to work with them. Otherwise, Lupe and Pepita were on their own, because their parents left their home early in the morning so they could be set up on the sidewalk by the time the first passersby came along; Lupe's mother was usually home by eight at night, but her father's spot was further away, and it took him more than an hour to get home. Sometimes the girls begged their parents to stay home with them—but they knew if their mother and father didn't work all day, every day, the family wouldn't be able to pay the rent or buy enough food to keep them alive.

Sometimes, Lupe used to tell her little sister stories about going to live with Tío Pedro and Tía Elena in *los Estados Unidos*—the United States—but they were only stories. Lupe didn't think they'd ever really come true. Lupe's aunt and uncle had been living in the United States for years. Tío Pedro had a job in a factory in Chicago, and he and his family had a nice house with three separate bedrooms, a living room, and a kitchen; they even had another room in their basement where Lupe's cousins played games and watched television. Lupe's mother had read her aunt's letter out loud, but Lupe couldn't really imagine what it would be like to live in such a big house. She knew her aunt and uncle had invited Lupe's family to come stay with them so they could become Americans too, but that had been years ago. The Ortegas had put their names on a list, and now they were waiting their turn. They had been waiting so long that Lupe hadn't believed they would ever really leave Mexico.

Two years ago, though, everything changed in the Ortegas' lives. Their names were on the list of people who could enter the United States. Tío Pedro sent them money for the airplane, and they flew all the way to Chicago, Illinois.

Now, Lupe lives with her family in a house with two bedrooms. Her father works in the factory where Tío Pedro works, and her mother works in a store. The whole family is

A sidewalk vendor in Mexico unpacks her wares for a day of sales.

learning English, and they are working hard to become American citizens. Lupe knows her family doesn't have as much money as many of the other students at the school she and Pepita attend—but she still remembers what it was like when the four of them lived in one room. She feels sad and angry when other kids make fun of the way she talks or the way she dresses, and sometimes she's homesick for the children she grew up with back in Mexico City. But she plans to work hard, just like her mother and father do, so that one day they'll have as much money as any other American.

The City of Tijuana

Perched on the border between Mexico and California, Tijuana is constantly growing. As many as 65,000 people are added to its population each year; many of these are people who have moved to Tijuana from other parts of Mexico, hoping for greater opportunities in the city's factories and tourist industry. The newcomers are expanding the city's boundaries by about eight acres a day.

The city's housing, roads, running water, and other public services can't keep up with the demand. Some poor families get electricity by hooking up illegal lines that can cause fires. When your house is made from cardboard and plywood, a fire can wipe out everything you own in mere minutes.

Pancho Espinoza grew up in a dump. He and his parents and brothers and sisters lived in tiny shack made from plastic garbage bags, a few old pieces of plywood, and a cardboard box, the kind a refrigerator comes in. Their skin was always gritty from the smoke that hung in a constant haze over the burning piles of garbage; some days they could barely see the sun.

The entire Espinoza family made their living sifting through Tijuana's trash. Every day they carried home bags of aluminum cans, wood, and clothing, some to sell and some to

Tijuana is full of desperately poor people. This overflow duct for the Tijuana River is home to several families.

Tijuana's sprawling suburbs

***foraged**: wandered in search of food.*

use. Their entire lives were linked to trash: they wore clothes from the dump, and they even ***foraged*** for food there. Pancho remembers how happy his parents would be when they found a bag of cloth diapers that could be washed and sold or electronics parts that would bring money from the shops downtown. What Pancho liked best was finding food: yogurt with expired dates that was still edible; half-rotten fruit; packages of stale, sweet cookies.

It was the only life Pancho had ever known. He never expected it to change. But when he was eleven, everything fell apart for his family. His father was run over by one of the immense garbage trucks that trundled into the dump. The driver

Trash Economy

About 1,200 tons of trash are carried into the Tijuana dump each day by enormous trucks. The people who make their living from the trash see these trucks as carrying fresh opportunities. The scavengers earn between $100 and $150 a month from the used clothing, aluminum, and wood pallets they pull out of the trash.

Dump scavengers don't need any special skills to make a living, they don't have to invest in anything, and the source of their livelihood is delivered to them every day. But they often pay a steep price for their precarious economics.

Most Mexican dump scavengers have a life expectancy of only thirty-nine years, compared to the Mexican general population's sixty-seven years. Diseases are prevalent in scavenger communities; untreated sewage, decaying food, and discarded medical needles are hosts to at least thirty different types of microbes. Toxic substances are also common amid the garbage—and too often they end up in the trash pickers' eyes and circulatory systems, and on their skin.

Many scavengers, however, can't get better jobs because they don't have high school diplomas or valid forms of identification, such as birth certificates. They have been rejected by much of society; trash gives them the only security they have ever known.

Mexico is full of children whose parents are too poor to care for them.

just kept on going; he never even knew the body of Pancho's father lay crushed in the load of garbage the truck left behind.

Without Pancho's father, the family started to disintegrate. His older brothers began selling and using drugs. His mother could not earn enough money to keep them all fed. In desperation, she finally packed up Pancho and his little brother and took them to an orphanage.

The orphanage was filled with other boys like Pancho and his brother. None of them were true orphans; all of them came from families where the parents could no longer care for all their children. Pancho was angry that his sisters got to stay with his mother; he was angry that his father hadn't been smart enough to get out of the truck's way; he was angry with the orphanage workers; and he was angry with himself for not being old enough to make his own way in the world, the way his older brothers were doing.

As soon, as Pancho was old enough to get a job, he ran away from the orphanage. On a moonless night, he crept across the border to *El Otro Lado* (The Other Side, a phrase used by Mexicans to refer to the United States). Border Patrol officers almost caught him, and as he dashed for cover, he gouged his face on the barbed-wire fence that marked the line between Mexico and the United States. Bleeding, terrified, he managed to make his way to San Ysidro, California, and from there he drifted south to Los Angeles.

Today he still lives in Los Angeles. He has married and has children of his own now; his wife works as a maid in a rich family's home, and he works as a mechanic in a garage. He still bears a deep scar across his face where the barbed wire tore his skin.

"Don't you get in any trouble," Pancho's wife warns him on Friday nights when he goes to the bar with some of the other men from work. "Don't let your temper get the best of you."

This boy lives in an orphanage while his parents are in prison.

Even if an undocumented alien lives for most of his life in the United States, he can be deported for committing a crime, as this man was.

Pancho still feels angry inside a lot of the time. Life doesn't seem fair to him. But he knows if he were ever to be picked up by the police for even the smallest reason, he would immediately be on his way back to Mexico. After all, he's an illegal immigrant.

So Pancho controls his temper the best he can. He doesn't want to lose everything he's built for himself and his family. They may not be rich by American standards—but they don't earn their living from picking through other people's garbage, and they have enough money to take care of their own children. That's all Pancho really cares about.

George Elizondo, Lupe Ortega, and Pancho Espinoza are all Mexican Americans. Like every other Mexican American, they have their own unique stories. Some have lived on the land that is now America's Southwest for hundreds of years, longer than many Anglo-Americans. Others are more recent immigrants whose families moved north looking for opportunity and security. Some are here legally; some aren't. But almost all are hardworking people who contribute to the American economy. What's more, they bring with them an ancient and colorful heritage that enriches American culture.

Habla Español

Estados Unidos (ace-tah-does oo-nee-does): United States

basura (bah-so-rah): garbage

2

Two Worlds

Long, long ago, the First People entered our world from the Lower World. Playing his flute, the Locust led them up from that other dimension through a narrow opening called a *sipapu*. These First People to enter our reality were the Anasazi, the Ancient Ones. They built elaborate multistoried buildings among the cliffs of what is now southern Utah, southwestern Colorado, northwestern New Mexico, and northern Arizona. Their cities would last for hundreds of years.

Ruins of a kiva, with a sipapu in the floor.

domesticated: *tamed.*

These ancient people learned to grow corn and other crops, like beans and squash. They ***domesticated*** the turkey and supplemented their diet with wild plants and game. Skilled artists, the Ancient Ones created beautiful pottery decorated with intricate patterns. But eventually, their life changed. A drought may have struck their land, or they may have simply overworked the soil; in any case, by A.D. 1300, they had abandoned the area. They moved into other parts of what is today the Southwest, and their descendants built other communities. There they lived for hundreds of years, their way of life changing very little.

The Sipapu

Different Native groups have different ideas about where the original opening into the Lower World is located, but they agree that today many sipapus can act as passageways to the other world. These doorways look like small holes in the floors of *kivas* (round, ceremonial structures). Special bodies of water or even special places in the landscape can also act as doors into the spiritual world. All these sipapus are the means of communication with the spirits.

When a person dies, she travels into the spirit world through the sipapu. Once long ago, death was not a permanent condition, for the sipapu could be traveled both ways; the dead could reemerge after a few days, and their bodies would revive. Native history tells how Coyote covered the sipapu with a stone, and now only spirits can pass back and forth through sipapus.

One of the Anasazi's cave dwellings in Mesa Verde, Arizona

Another Ancient Culture

Meanwhile, far to the south, another culture was thriving among the mountains that curled down the continent toward the narrow strip of land that connected the two great landmasses. Between A.D. 1200 and 1500, the Mexica people had united the land into a mighty empire. All the tribes that formed this empire were together known as "Aztecs." The stories they told about their deepest roots were not so different from that of the Anasazi to the north.

According to the oldest Aztec history, the Mexica people had originally crawled from the bowels of the earth through seven caves. They then settled in Aztlan, the "Place of Whiteness." Some modern-day historians speculate that Aztlan was located in the American Southwest, in the same location as the original sipapu from which the Ancient Ones emerged from the Under World.

In any case, the Mexica migrated southward. They journeyed for centuries, gaining in strength and military power as they searched for a home, a land where they could settle permanently. Down through the years, they waited for a sign that would tell them when they should cease their travels and claim their home.

One of the Mexica leaders received a vision: a great eagle with a snake in its mouth would mark their permanent home. Finally, in 1325, after centuries of wandering, the Mexica's migration came to an end when they saw a prickly pear cactus growing on an island in the middle of Lake Texcoco. Upon it was a great eagle, with a snake in its mouth. This was

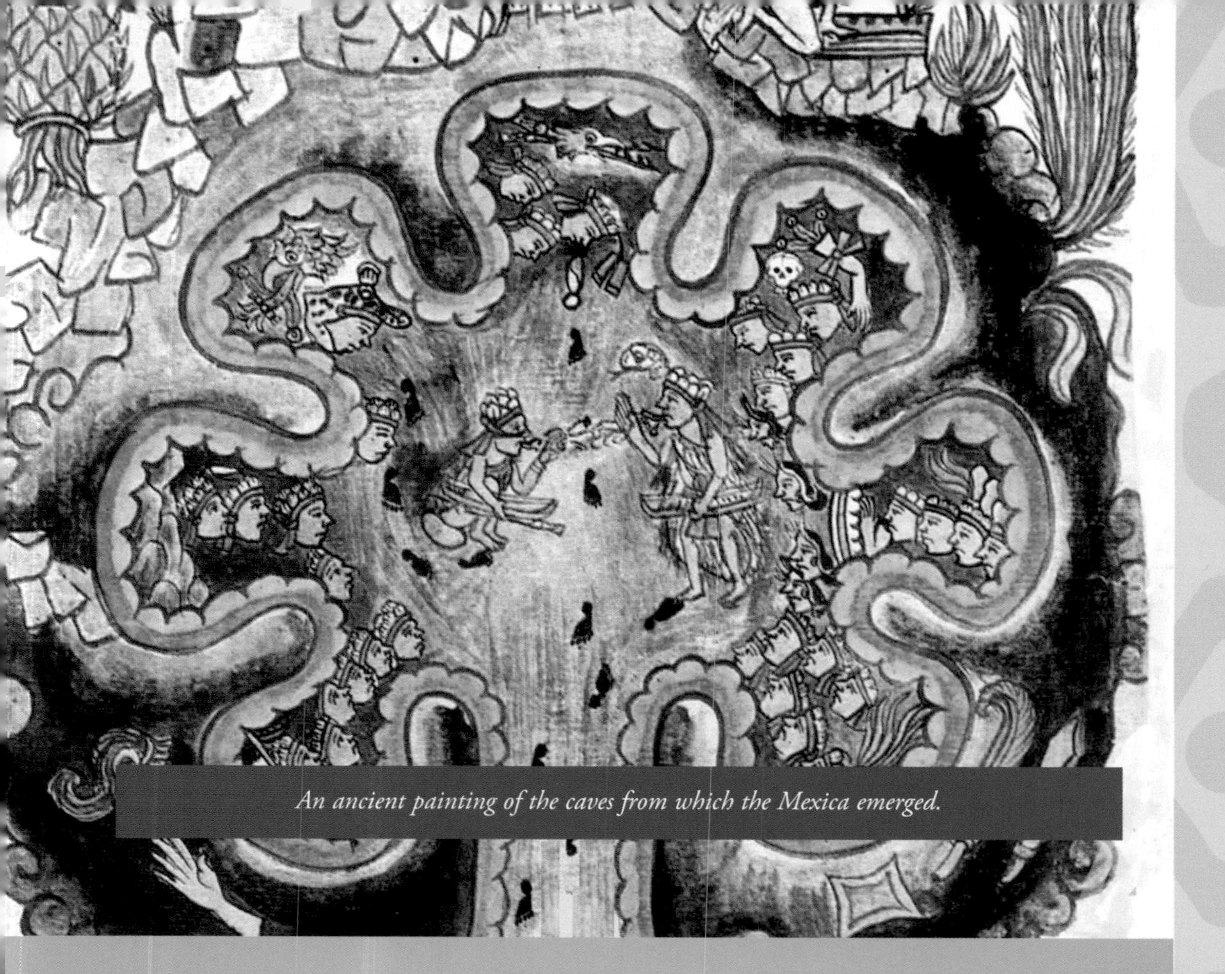

An ancient painting of the caves from which the Mexica emerged.

Shared Roots

The Native people of Mexico speak *Nahuatl*, a language that is very similar to that spoken by the Hopi, Pima, Yaqui, and Kiowa to the north, and the Maya to the south. These linguistic similarities tell historians that these separate groups of people probably share common long-ago roots.

Aztec drawing of the founding of Tenochtitlan

the exact sign the god Huitzilopochtli had revealed would mark their permanent home, and this would be the site of their capital, Tenochtitlan. From here, they conquered and ruled the neighboring tribes.

Another World

While the Anasazi and the Aztec were building their cultures in the Western Hemisphere, across the ocean, in a faraway land, other societies were gaining strength. One of these was Castile, the largest kingdom at that time in the part of Europe called the Iberian Peninsula.

The Olmecs

The Aztecs were not the first people to thrive in Mexico. Before the arrival of the Mexica, the Olmecs dwelled there for thousands of years, since 2000 B.C. The Olmecs' civilization was a sophisticated one; they developed systems of numbering, writing, and keeping track of weeks and months. They are believed to be the first people in the Americas to develop religious centers, and they built pyramids that bring to mind the ancient civilization of Egypt. Their rich culture earned them the title of "mother culture" for the generations of Native people who came after them. Although the Olmecs had disappeared by 400 B.C., their heritage continues to play a role in the culture of modern-day Mexicans and Mexican Americans. They also made many lasting contributions to today's world. For example, one of North America's favorite sports—basketball—comes from the rubber-ball game played by these ancient people.

The Eastern and Western Hemispheres

Looking from outer space, we all inhabit an enormous blue sphere—our Earth. If we divide this globe by cutting it in half from top to bottom, we can imagine hemispheres. ("Hemi" means half, and a sphere is round, so a hemisphere is half of something round, in this case, the globe.) The Eastern Hemisphere contains Africa, Australia, Europe, and Asia. People who come from this part of the world sometimes call it the "Old World." The Western Hemisphere consists of what we today call the "Americas." Once people in the Eastern Hemisphere became aware of it, they called the Western Hemisphere the "New World." Yet it was hardly new to the millions of people who had lived there for thousands of years. For more than 15,000 years, the cultures of the Western Hemisphere had flourished, and in all this time, the Eastern and Western halves of planet Earth had lived in ignorance of each other's existence.

The Iberian Peninsula straddles the Mediterranean Sea and the Atlantic Ocean, which means that it lies between Europe and Africa. Earlier, Muslims from Africa had moved into the Iberian Peninsula's population, but over the centuries, the Christian kingdoms of Castile, Aragon, and Portugal had pushed the Islamic forces back toward the Mediterranean. At the same time, the Christian kingdoms warred among themselves.

Isabella was a headstrong princess who lived in Castile, where she and her brothers vied for power in the kingdom. When her brother Fernando died, his troops made her their leader. Isabella knew the conflict was harming Castile, so she made a deal with her half-brother Henry: "Declare me heir to the throne and we will make peace." Henry agreed.

In 1469, Isabella planned to marry Prince Ferdinand, heir to the throne of the neighboring kingdom of Aragon. He was "handsome in face, body and person," known for breaking women's hearts and fighting valiantly in battle. Ferdinand's father, the King of Aragon, was thrilled at the idea of his son marrying into the royal family of Castile, since that kingdom was much larger than his.

The marriage seemed like a good idea—but not to Isabella's half-brother Henry. When Henry heard Isabella might marry Ferdinand, he was furious because Aragon had long been his enemy. Henry ordered troops to prevent Ferdinand from meeting Isabella. The Prince of Aragon, as clever as he was courageous, sneaked into the kingdom in disguise. With the help of the Archbishop of Toledo, Ferdinand and Isabella eloped.

Their marriage made history. By uniting Castile and Aragon, they created the nation known today as Spain. The newly united Spanish nation became a world superpower.

Deeply religious, Isabella and Ferdinand were known as the "Catholic Royalty." Just a few years after they became King and

Pope: the worldwide leader of the Catholic Church.

heretics: people who have beliefs that contradict established religious teachings.

prejudices: opinions about a particular group that are based on incomplete and sometimes incorrect information.

Queen, Ferdinand and Isabella asked the ***Pope*** for permission to create a new government office in Spain—the Inquisition. Under the Inquisition, Jews and Muslims had three choices—convert to Christianity, leave Spain, or be tortured to death. Enormous crowds rushed to the ports of Spain, fleeing for their lives. Not all escaped. More than 30,000 Jews, Muslims, and other "***heretics***" were tortured and killed by the Spanish Inquisition. These violent ***prejudices*** would follow the Spaniards when they crossed the ocean to the New World in the Western Hemisphere.

The atmosphere of pride and religion also created a special breed of men—conquistadors, soldiers who fought for their religion, while gaining lands for Spain. These men would lead the invasion of the Americas.

Habla Español

iglesia (ee-glace-ee-ah): church

rey (ray): king

reina (ray-ee-nah): queen

Religious Competition

In 1517, a German monk named Martin Luther began to voice disagreements he had with the Catholic leader, the Pope. This led to the splitting of the Catholic Church. Those who left the Church were known as Protestants, or Reformers—and this time in history is sometimes known as the Reformation.

Spanish Catholic leaders in the 1500s looked at the world as a four-way religious competition. They were determined to defeat Muslims, Jews, and Protestants whatever way they could. This sense of religious competition influenced the conquest of the Americas in two ways. First, Spain wanted to claim all the land it could for the Catholic Church, and second, the religious wars in Europe required gold and silver from the New World to finance armies back in Spain.

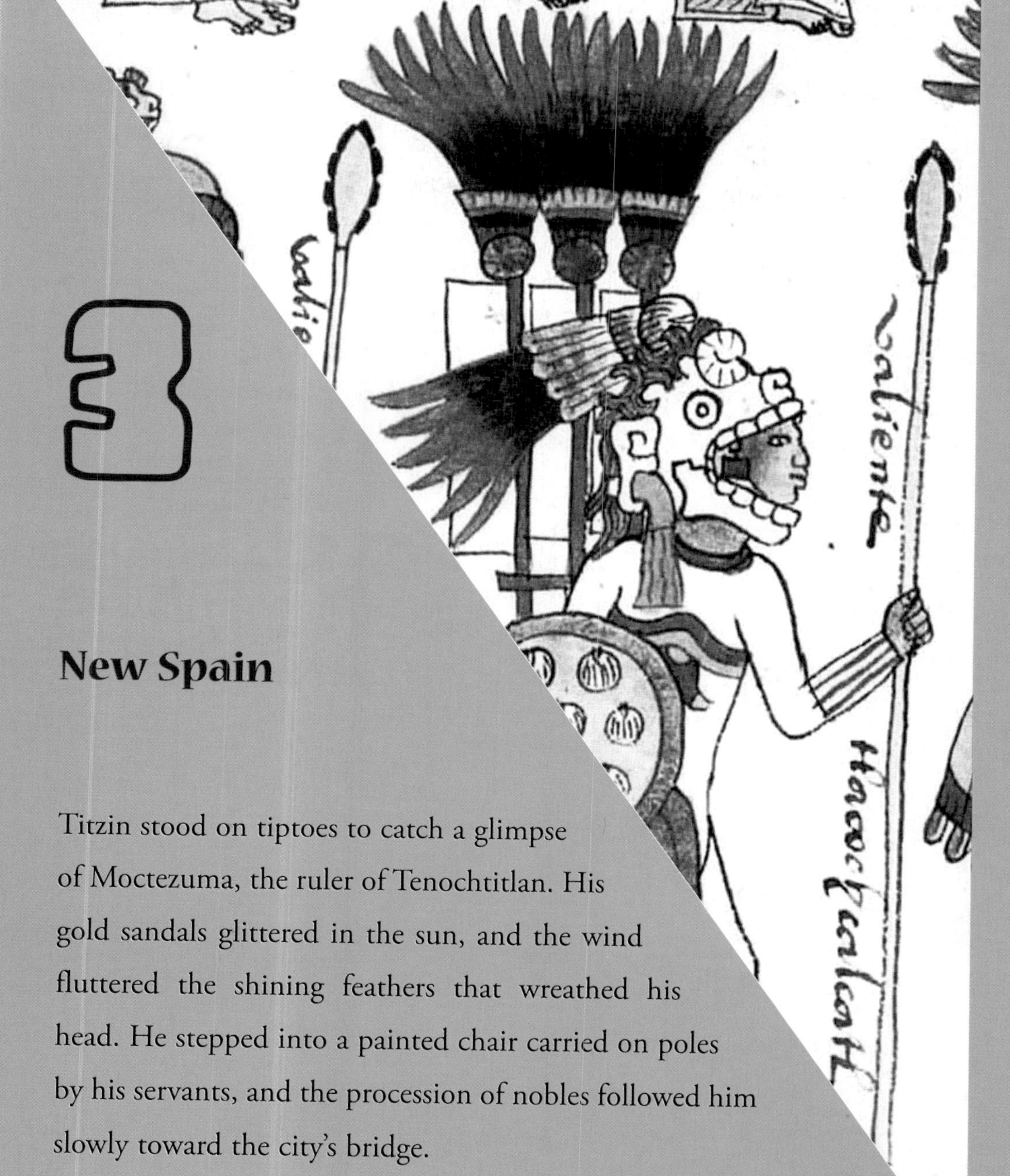

3

New Spain

Titzin stood on tiptoes to catch a glimpse of Moctezuma, the ruler of Tenochtitlan. His gold sandals glittered in the sun, and the wind fluttered the shining feathers that wreathed his head. He stepped into a painted chair carried on poles by his servants, and the procession of nobles followed him slowly toward the city's bridge.

For days, the city had buzzed with news of the mysterious pale-skinned strangers who had landed on the coast to the east and were traveling toward Tenochtitlan. They were rumored to be gods, perhaps even Quetzalcoatl, the greatest of the gods, returning at last to his people. They were said to carry strange magical logs that thundered and threw fiery death.

Titzin used her elbows to keep her place at the front of the crowd that followed after the procession as it crawled along the road. She had never seen a god before, and she was determined to see for herself what these strangers were like.

And then there they were: the strangers came across the bridge to meet Moctezuma and his nobles. The gods rode beasts Titzin had never seen, and they were dressed from head to toe in shiny metal that glittered in the sunlight. On the tops of their long spears, bright banners rippled in the wind. Behind them walked thousands of warriors.

"Tlaxcalla!" muttered the man next to Titzin, his voice full of loathing. The Tlaxcalla were longtime enemies of the Mexica.

What did it mean? Titzin wondered. Were these strangers really gods? Now that they had reached Tenochtitlan, the center of the world, what would they do? Titzin shivered, and her excitement dimmed, as though a shadow had passed over the sun. She had an uneasy feeling that life was about to change.

Some twenty years later, in the land to the north, a boy named Awa watched while other white-skinned strangers rode into his community. Like the men Titzin had seen, these strangers wore metal armor and rode upon strange beasts that pranced and snorted. Awa's people, the Zuni, did not think the strangers were gods, however. They recognized warriors when they saw them, and they quickly prepared to defend their homes.

Awa heard that the strange men had come looking for cities of gold. He knew that the mud houses of his people sometimes glittered like gold when the rays of the setting sun shone on them just right, and he chuckled to himself. Stupid white faces, mistaking mud and sunlight for gold. And why were they so interested in gold anyway? It was a pretty stone, true, but the Earth had many pretty stones to offer.

Awa knew his people were brave and strong. He never doubted they would drive away the foolish white faces.

Quetzalcoatl

Quetzalcoatl (which means "the Plumed Serpent") was the creator of human life. Long ago, he was said to have come down from the sun and visited the Mexica, bringing with him words of wisdom on how they should live their lives. He opposed both human sacrifice and warfare, and he encouraged people to devote themselves instead to self-discipline and the creation of beautiful things. He was said to have white skin, and he was considered to be a god of life, perhaps even the Creator of the entire world.

Because his words overturned the status quo and made him many enemies among the ruling class, he was murdered. After he was put to death, however, he rose from the dead. His heart became the morning star, and he himself became young again. He left this world, but he promised to return again.

Some anthropologists and theologians have drawn comparisons between Christ's story and Quetzalcoatl's. Others point out, however, that by the time of the Spanish conquest, the Aztecs had transformed Quetzalcoatl into a military deity in whose name they committed human sacrifices. However, the same could be said of the founder of Christianity; he claimed to be the god of love, and yet for centuries, his name has been invoked as a reason for wars and massacres.

Nothing to Fear?

Miguel Leon-Portilla, a Mexican anthropologist, gathered firsthand accounts written by the Aztecs who were alive at the time of Cortés's arrival in Tenochtitlan. According to these accounts (found in *Broken Spears: The Aztec Account of the Conquest of Mexico*, 1962), these are the words that Moctezuma and Cortés spoke to each other that day:

> The king . . . stood up to welcome Cortés; he came forward, bowed his head low and addressed him in these words: "Our lord, you are weary. The journey has tired you, but now you have arrived on the earth. You have come to your city, Mexico. You have come here to sit on your throne, to sit under its canopy. . . . No, it is not a dream. I am not walking in my sleep. . . . I have seen you at last! . . . You have come out of the clouds and mists to sit on your throne again. This was foretold . . . and now it has taken place. You have come back to us; you have come down from the sky. Rest now, and take possession of your royal houses. Welcome to your land, my lords!"
>
> . . . Cortés replied in his strange and savage tongue, speaking first to [his translator]: "Tell Moctezuma that we are his friends. There is nothing to fear. We have wanted to see him for a long time. . . . Tell him that we love him well and that our hearts are contented." Then he said to Moctezuma: "We have come to your house in Mexico as friends. There is nothing to fear."

Taos Pueblo in New Mexico has been inhabited for hundreds of years, longer than any European U.S. city.

The Pueblo

When the Spanish saw the elaborate communities the Native people had built for themselves in the American Southwest, they named these people the Pueblo (pronounced "pway-blow," the Spanish word for village). Historians estimate that there were probably as many as a hundred pueblos at the time of their first encounter with the Spanish; today nineteen pueblos remain, including (among others) Zuni, Hopi, Acoma, and Taos.

The Spanish brought a new religion to the Pueblo people.

A World Changed Forever

Titzin's and Awa's lives would never be the same again after the white men's arrival. Most of their friends and family would either die or be enslaved. In less than a century, the invasion was completed. From Awa's home down through Titzin's, thousands of Native people were killed by disease or battle. All this land was now part of *Nueva España*—New Spain.

First Contact in the Southwest

While Hernando Cortés was the conquistador who conquered the Aztecs, another Spaniard, Francisco Hernández de Córdoba, was the first to encounter the Pueblo. He and his troops quickly clashed with the people, forcing them to flee from their homes. In 1598, the first Spanish capital was established in what is now New Mexico. The Spanish colonization of the American Southwest had officially begun.

When the conquistadors from Spain could not get their hands on as much gold as they had hoped to find, they looked for other ways to gain riches from the New World. They built huge farms, *haciendas*, where they grew great quantities of crops; they mined the land for silver and copper, as well as gold; and they stripped the trees from the land so they could raise cattle. To do all this work, they needed a labor source—and so they turned to the Native people for slaves.

All across the Western Hemisphere, the story was similar: the coming of the Europeans brought death and destruction to the Native cultures that had lived there for thousands of years. For the Native Americans, contact with Europe was the beginning of a battle for cultural survival that continues even today. Historians who have studied the

genocide: the systematic killing of all the people from a national, ethnic, or religious group.

stigma: the shame or disgrace attached to something regarded as socially unacceptable.

A Terrible Statistic

No one knows for sure how many Native people died after the Europeans' arrival, but an average estimate is around 40 million in the first hundred years.

number of Native American deaths following contact with Europe conclude that it may be history's worst case of ***genocide***. Although many were murdered by the European invaders, many more died from diseases to which they had no immunity.

A New Race

But things went a little differently in the Spanish colonies than they did in the English colonies to the north and east. Despite the Spaniards' reputation for coldhearted cruelty, they did not completely wipe out entire civilizations the way the Englishmen did. Instead, the Spanish readily adopted whatever elements of Mexican society were compatible with their own, leaving the basic culture in place. What's more, few Spanish women accompanied the conquistadors, so many Spanish men turned to Native women for their mates. Although they certainly had their share of prejudices, the Spanish, unlike the English, were accustomed to a society where dark-skinned people (the Islamic Moors, originally from Africa) mixed freely with those with lighter skin; as a result, not as much ***stigma*** was attached to intermarriage. The Spaniards in Mexico blended with the Native people to create an entirely new culture.

This new culture was a blend of Native and Spanish, with the strengths and richness of both. One of the most long-lasting fruits of this union was the Mexican version of Christianity.

Miguel Leon-Portilla provides this firsthand account of the killing in Tenochtitlan:

> [In the midst of a celebration], they were all put to death. The dancers and singers were completely unarmed. They had brought only their embroidered cloaks, their turquoises, their lip plugs, their necklaces, their clusters of heron feathers, their trinkets made of deer hooves. Those who played the drums, the old men, had brought their gourds of snuff and their timbrels.
>
> The Spaniards attacked the musicians first, slashing at their hands and faces until they had killed all of them. The singers—and even the spectators—were also killed. This slaughter . . . went on for three hours. Then the Spaniards burst into the rooms of the temple to kill the others: those who were carrying water, or bringing fodder to the horses, or grinding meal, or sweeping, or standing watch over this work.
>
> The king Moctezuma . . . protested: "Our lords, that is enough! What are you doing? These people . . . are completely unarmed!"

La Raza

Today, many Mexican Americans speak of "la Raza," a term that refers to all descendants of the Spanish–Native encounter in the Americas. The term is a way of claiming their distinct cultural heritage, while looking toward the future with pride and hope. "La Raza is the affirmation of the most basic ingredient of our personality," writes José Angel Gutiérrez, "the brownhood of our Indian ancestors wedded to all the other skin colors of mankind. . . . As children of La Raza, we are heirs of a spiritual and biological miracle."

Missionaries and Miracles

Ironically, the Spanish conquistadors took their religion very seriously. They murdered, raped, and cheated the Native people—and yet they were determined to make them Christians. They asked the Pope to send missionaries to teach the Natives, and he readily complied.

Although the missionaries' chief goal was to introduce the Indians to Christian doctrine, in many ways these religious men and women laid the groundwork for the ***fusion*** of the Spanish and Mexican cultures. The Native people saw little in the conquistadors' lives that attracted them—but many missionaries won the Natives' trust by doing what they could to protect them from the conquistadors' cruelty. The missionaries learned the Indian languages and established schools where children could learn to read and write. They taught the adults European methods in farming, masonry, carpentry, ironwork, weaving, dying, and ceramics.

According to many Native traditions, people were expected to adopt the religion of conquering tribes. As a result, some Indians did not resist conversion to Christianity. Similarities between Christianity's rituals and their own helped make the process go more smoothly. Even the Aztec practice of human sacrifice, so horrifying to the Spaniards, helped many Natives accept the concept of eating the body and blood of Christ in the ***Eucharist.***

But one event alone is most responsible for Mexican Christianity: the miraculous appearance of a dark-skinned Virgin Mary to a poor Indian in December of 1531.

Soon after the miracle's occurrence, the events were recorded by an Indian named Don Antonio Valeriano, an educated man who had converted to Christianity. He wrote his account in Náhuatl, the language of the Aztecs. The story is called the "Nican Mopohua" because those are the very words written in the manuscript. ("Nican Mopohua" means "Here it is told.") Here is Don Valeriano's story:

> Juan Diego was a poor Indian that used to walk around the land that now surrounds Mexico City. . . . One day . . . he

fusion: *the merging of two or more things.*

Eucharist: *a ceremony in many Christian churches in which blessed bread and wine or fruit juice are symbolically turned into the body and blood of Jesus Christ.*

The Evangelization of Mexico

The first Catholic missionaries arrived in Mexico in 1523 and 1524. By 1559 there were 300 Franciscan friars at eighty missions throughout Nueva España. They were followed by the other religious orders. Altogether some 12,000 churches were built during the three centuries of Spanish rule over Mexico.

The Spanish priests worked to bring Christianity to Native people.

> heard music, and smelled a sweet perfume coming from a small hill nearby. Somebody, in a very friendly voice, was calling his name: "Juanito, Juan Dieguito." He climbed the Tepeyac hill and he saw a young woman standing there. She asked him to come closer.
>
> When he was in front of her he saw how magnificent she was: Her clothes had a light like that of the sun, and she was very beautiful.

According to tradition, the woman was dark skinned, like the Native people of the Americas, and she spoke to Juan Diego in Nahuatl. She said to him, "Know for sure, my dearest son, that I am . . . the Virgin Mary, Mother of the One Great God of Truth who gives us life. I am truly your Compassionate Mother, yours and of all the people who live together in this land." She told Juan Diego to build her a "sacred little house" on this site, "because there I will listen to their weeping . . . to remedy, to cleanse and nurse all their different troubles, their miseries, their suffering."

Don Valeriano's story continues:

> She . . . asked him to go to Mexico, to the Bishop's Palace, to tell him that she wanted a temple built . . . for her.
>
> He promised the Lady to obey her, and he walked all the way down to Mexico, to talk with the Bishop, Fray Juan de Zumárraga. In the palace, he had to wait for a while, but finally he was in the presence of the Bishop himself. He told him about all the marvelous things he had heard and seen, and then presented to him the request from the Queen of Heaven. The Bishop did not believe him, so he walked back to the Tepeyac

A street mural in Tijuana records Juan Diego's vision.

hill. And she was waiting there for him. As soon as he saw her, he said, "Lady, Queen, my little daughter, my little girl, I went there to fulfill your orders. The Governor Priest was kind to me, he listened to me, but I think he did not understand me; he did not believe me. So I beg you, my Lady, Queen, my little girl, that you send one of your noblemen; because I am a simple man, I am small, I am like a wood ladder, I need to be guided, so I will fail you, and I don't want you to be angry at me." She insisted in that he was the one that had to carry her orders; nobody else. He promised, again, to do as she said.

Next day, Sunday, he went to the Bishop again, and he repeated his story. The Bishop asked him a lot of questions, and finally said that, in order to build a temple, he needed a token, a tangible sign from the Lady.

A modern mural of the Virgin of Guadalupe portrays her holding a child dead from street violence.

Next day, Monday, Juan Diego did not meet the Lady, because his uncle, Juan Bernardino, was very ill, and he went to visit him. He spent the night there, and next morning, very early, Juan Diego started walking to Tlatelolco, in order to find a priest for his uncle, because he was sure of Juan Bernardino's near death. When he approached the little hill, he took a different turn, because he didn't want the Lady from Heaven to stop him; he was in a hurry. . . . But she suddenly appeared in front of him and asked him, "What happened, my little son? Where are you going?" He was embarrassed, and he said, "My young one, my little daughter, my girl, I hope you are happy; how are you this morning? Do you feel well?" And he told her that he was going to get a priest, because his uncle was dying. She answered: "Put this in your heart, my little son: do not be afraid. Am I not here, me, your mother? Are you not under my shadow, under my care? Am I not the fountain of joy? Are you not in the crease of my cloak, in the fold of my arms? Do you need anything else?" And she told him that his uncle was sound in that very moment. Then she told him to climb the hill and cut the flowers that were there. He did so, and was very amazed to find many beautiful flowers up there, because it was not the time for them. He cut the flowers and put them inside his *tilma* [a cloak] and then . . . she sent him to the Bishop, asking him to show what he carried.

When Juan Diego arrived at the palace, he had a long wait to see the Bishop. He told him all the story, about the Lady, the hill, the flowers, the orders from her. All this time he was holding his tilma, with the flowers inside. Finally, the Bishop asked him to show what he was carrying. When he opened his cloak, the flowers fell to the floor, and there, on the white fabric, was the image of the Lady from Heaven, Nuestra Señora de Guadalupe.

The Virgin's image appears in many places throughout Mexico and the United States.

A street mural expresses Mexico's unique spiritual beliefs that blend Christianity and Native religious imagery.

The Virgin's reported appearance convinced many Native Americans that the god of the Spaniards was also a deity who cared about them. They adopted Catholicism and made it their own—and they drew comfort and strength from it when the cruelty and oppression of the Spanish seemed overwhelming.

Mistreatment and Poverty

While the missionaries were busy converting, educating, and helping the Native people, the other Spaniards were establishing New Spain's political, social, and eco-

The Virgin of Guadalupe

Speaking in the Aztec language, the Virgin told Juan Diego her name was Coatlaxopeuh, which is pronounced "Quat-la-su-pay" and sounds similar to the Spanish word *Guadalupe*. For Spanish-speakers, the name reminded them of a place in Spain where there was already a shrine dedicated to the Virgin Mary. To this day, this miraculous vision is referred to as the appearance of "Our Lady of Guadalupe"—and Guadalupe has become a symbol of hope, courage, and identity for the Mexican people.

nomic structure. The *Ciudad de Mexico* (Mexico City) was erected on the ruins of the old Aztec capital, and the remainder of the conquered territory was gradually divvied up into grants for huge estates, known as *encomiendas*, operated under a ***feudal*** system by some five hundred Spanish landlords.

Supplies and communications moved north from Mexico City along the *El Camino Real*, the Royal Road that stretched

***feudal**: relating to the legal or social system in which tenants work land under lords in return for military service.*

Taos Pueblo today

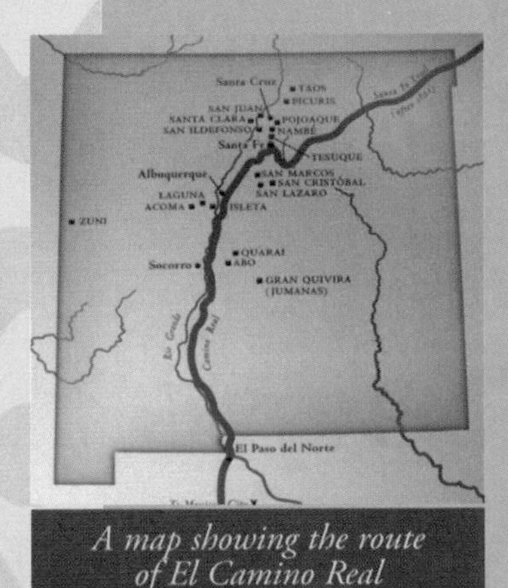

A map showing the route of El Camino Real

2,000 miles (3,220 km) to the land of the Pueblo, all the way to the new Spanish city of Santa Fe. Caravans of Spanish colonists made the six-month journey, bringing with them cattle and sheep and horses. They introduced new technologies to the Pueblo people, and at first, the two groups of people lived peacefully side by side.

Unlike many of the Indians to the south, however, the Pueblo were unwilling to accept the Spaniards' religion, and they resented the missionaries' attempts to rob them of their culture. Also, as more and more Spanish settlers moved into the area, the Indians were often forced into slavery. In 1680, the Pueblo's resentment boiled over into rebellion. Warriors overthrew the colonists, burned their churches, and killed their priests. When the Pueblo converged on Santa Fe, a thousand Spanish settlers streamed out of the city and fled south down El Camino Real.

For the next few years, warfare continued between the Pueblo and the Spanish. Eventually, as more and more Spanish came into the area from the south, the Pueblo were forced to accept their presence, just as the Aztec had in the lands to the south. New Spain was too powerful for them to resist.

Like the Aztec, many Natives in the American Southwest also interbred with the Spanish. Most of the children of these unions—called *mestizos*, or "mixed"—were as poor and oppressed as their Native parents. Mestizos and Natives bode their time, hoping that one day things would change.

The ancient land of the early Mexicans.

Habla Español

guerra (gayr-rah): war

camino (cah-mee-no): road

real (ray-ahl): royal

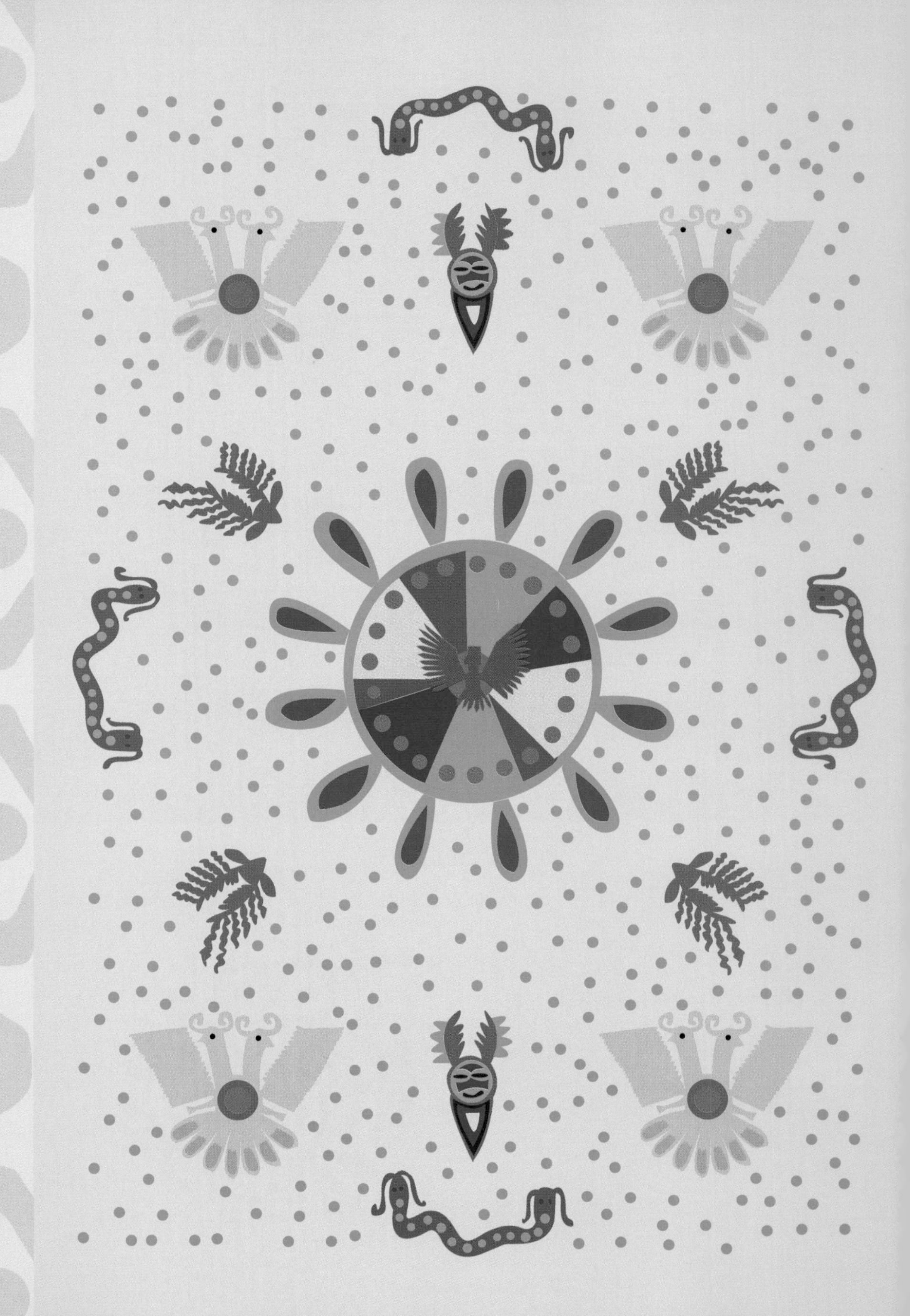

The Birth of the Mexican Nation

"The world is changing," Manuel Mendoza told his son in 1810. "Nothing will ever be the same."

Rafa Mendoza just nodded and went back to throwing sticks for his dog to chase. He'd been hearing about the world changing for as long as he'd been alive. For him, these changes were nothing new.

Spain's colonies stretched through much of North America as well as South America.

But for his parents and his grandparents, these upheavals were enormous. The old kingdoms that had ruled the world for hundreds of years were being shaken at their roots. Great Britain's colonies in North America had revolted and won their freedom—and now, some thirty years later, they were still on their own as an independent nation, the United States of America. France too had gone through a revolution of its own twenty-one years ago. News of these events had reached Spain's colonies in the Western Hemisphere, and new ideas had filtered into even the most remote areas. Now Spain's colonies had begun to revolt as well.

These events gave Rafa's family a sense of hope. The old days of oppression and heartache might be coming to an end. But the news of battles and bloodshed also frightened them. In a time of such instability and violence, they feared for their children. What sort of world would they inherit? If everything was turned upside down, would the Mendoza family emerge from the chaos safe and prosperous—or would they lose the little they had?

Rafa knew these questions worried his parents. Whenever news came to them from the outside world, his father, uncles, and grandfather would sit up late beside the fire, talking and thinking, worrying and hoping. The next day, his mother would have little lines between her eyebrows, and while she cooked and cleaned, she would murmur prayers to the Virgin.

But Rafa and his brother Victor were excited by all the talk of revolts and soldiers, courage and action. When they played together out in the hills behind their house, they took turns pretending they were Father Hidalgo, the brave priest who would bring them freedom from Spanish rule.

"The Spanish have had things their way for too long," Victor would say. "What gives them the right to tell us what to do?"

Rafa and his family had a Spanish name, and they spoke the Spanish language. But they also spoke Nahuatl, the ancient language of their land, and their blood tied them to the time long before the Europeans' arrival. "Mestizo" was the word some people used to describe Rafa and his family: mixed. Their ancestors had been both Indians and Spaniards—but today they were neither and both. Rafa and his family had never had a country to call their own.

The Shout of Pain

Father Hidalgo wasn't a mestizo like the Mendozas—he was a *criollo*, born in the Americas from pure European blood—but he believed all human beings were equal,

radical: reflecting extreme changes.

nationalism: proud loyalty and devotion to a country.

royalists: those who support a monarchy as the form of government.

no matter whether their ancestors came from the Western Hemisphere or the Eastern. Because of his ***radical*** beliefs, Hidalgo wanted freedom from Spain as much as the mestizos and Indians did.

News of his activity had reached Rafa's family; leading a ragtag horde of mestizos and Indians, Hidalgo was marching toward Mexico City, the heart of Spanish power in North America. Over their heads fluttered the banner of the Virgin of Guadalupe, the new symbol of Mexican ***nationalism***. The nation of Mexico did not yet exist, but it had become an idea in the hearts and minds of Hidalgo's followers.

The tide of revolution had risen to a crest on September 16, 1810, when Father Hidalgo had stood in his little church in the small village of Dolores and shouted, "Long live our Lady of Guadalupe! Down with bad government! Death to the Spaniards!" His words would go down in history as the *Grito de Delores* (Cry of Sorrows). They spurred thousands of people to take action, people like the Mendozas, Indians and mestizos who had been poor and oppressed their entire lives. By the time they neared Mexico City, some 50,000 people had joined forces to march against their Spanish rulers.

The Ongoing Revolution

Historians today believe Father Hidalgo could have successfully taken the city, ousting the Spaniards from control—but for some reason, he hesitated and turned back. The tide now turned in the opposite direction; the ***royalists*** pursued

Mexican Americans celebrate their Independence Day with parades and parties.

Mexican Independence Day

Although Mexican independence would not be achieved until more than a decade after Father Hidalgo's call for rebellion, the Diez y Seis de Septiembre (Sixteenth of September) is celebrated as Mexico's Independence Day.

A young criollo woman

the rebels, and many of Hidalgo's followers abandoned him. Eventually, the brave priest was trapped, tried for treason, and executed.

But the revolution did not die. Another priest, José Morelos, one of Hidalgo's students, took over where Hidalgo had left off. Unlike Father Hidalgo, Morelos possessed military and political know-how; he trained his troops, assembled a ***congress***, and set about writing a ***constitution***. The document, formally issued in 1814, committed the revolution to equality for all.

Unfortunately, not everyone approved of Morelos' ideas. Many of the criollos, the wealthy Spaniards who had been born in North America, did not want to recognize mestizos and Indians as their equals. They withdrew their support from the revolution, and once again, the royalist forces gained power. They swept against the rebel movement, and in 1815, Morelos was captured, tried, and executed. This time there was no one to pick up the leadership of the rebel movement. The revolutionaries retreated into the mountains, and the Spanish government regained almost complete control of the colony.

Six years later, however, Spain was reeling from rebellion at home. The Mexican criollos feared they would lose their privileged positions if a more liberal government took control of Spain, and so, for very different reasons than the earlier revolution, the criollos pushed for independence from Spain. This time they got it. Led by Augustín de Iturbide, an army officer, Mexico declared itself an independent nation. Iturbide's forces joined with the remnants of the earlier revolutionary movement, uniting under a slogan referred to as the Three Guarantees: independence, religion, and equality. A year later, Iturbide was ***inaugurated*** Emperor of Mexico.

But the forces that had supported independence were sim-

congress: *a formal meeting of delegates or representatives to discuss matters of concern.*

constitution: *a written set of laws and principles that rule a country.*

inaugurated: *sworn into office.*

factions: subgroups with their own interests and beliefs that are not always the same as those of the larger group.

coup: the sudden overthrow of a government, usually in a violent manner by the military.

exiled: forced to leave the country, often for political reasons.

ply too divided to shape a solid government. While the criollos wanted to keep their wealth and position, the mestizos and Indians wanted true equality and a new economic structure that would allow them to prosper. Iturbide lacked the strength to control the divided ***factions***. In 1823, after only a year in power, he was removed from office by a revolutionary ***coup***. The new president who took his place as leader of Mexico was a young criollo officer named Antonio Lopez de Santa Anna.

Ongoing Conflict

Santa Anna's original goal was to rid the country of Spaniards. As his ambition grew, however, he began seizing more and more power. He appointed himself president and was in and out of office eleven times between 1833 and 1855.

Meanwhile, as settlers from the United States began moving into northern Mexico, they talked of establishing their own country, independent of Mexico. By 1834, the Americans outnumbered the Mexicans in the northern part of Mexico. In 1835, these settlers declared their independence.

But Santa Anna was never one to give in without a fight. He attacked the Americans at the Alamo, defeating them soundly. At a later battle in San Jacinto, however, the Americans defeated the Mexicans and captured Santa Anna. He was forced to sign the Velasco Agreement in 1836, giving northern Mexico its freedom.

Mexico, furious over this loss, ***exiled*** Santa Anna and refused to recognize the Velasco Agreement. For nine years, this area in

Mexican forces won the Alamo but lost the war.

The lives of all Mexican Americans today have been shaped by the events of the nineteenth century.

northern Mexico was in limbo. It considered itself a free state, but Mexico still considered it part of the country. Finally, the United States admitted the land into the Union, and it became the state of Texas.

In response, Mexico declared war on the United States. The Mexican government reconciled with Santa Anna and asked him to lead the war against the United States. The United States troops, led by General Zachary Taylor, were better prepared for battle than the Mexicans, and American forces captured Mexico City on September 14, 1847; the Mexican-American War was officially over on February 2, 1848, when the Treaty of Guadalupe Hidalgo was signed. This treaty called for Mexico to turn over all land north of the Rio Grande River (Texas), as well as all the land from the Gila River to the Pacific

Ocean (what is now California, Nevada, Utah, and Arizona, as well as parts of Wyoming, Colorado, and New Mexico).

Despite Santa Anna's military failures, Mexico allowed him to name himself dictator of Mexico. In order to raise funds for the military, he sold additional land to the United States—a piece of Mexico along the Gila River (present-day Arizona and New Mexico). This deal, called the Gadsden Purchase, was the last major change of Mexican boundary lines. Mexico had lost over 50 percent of its territory to the United States in just a few short years.

Whether they now lived in the United States or south of the new boundary lines, the years that followed were hard ones for the Mexican people. Many changes had indeed taken place in the lives of ordinary Mexicans like Rafa Mendoza; unfortunately, not all were positive ones. Through a succession of Mexican and American presidents, the Mexican economy limped along—and poor people paid the price for politicians' lack of wisdom and justice.

Habla Español

grito (gree-toe): shout, cry

delores (day-lore-aise): sorrows, pains

dolares (doe-lahr-ace): dollars

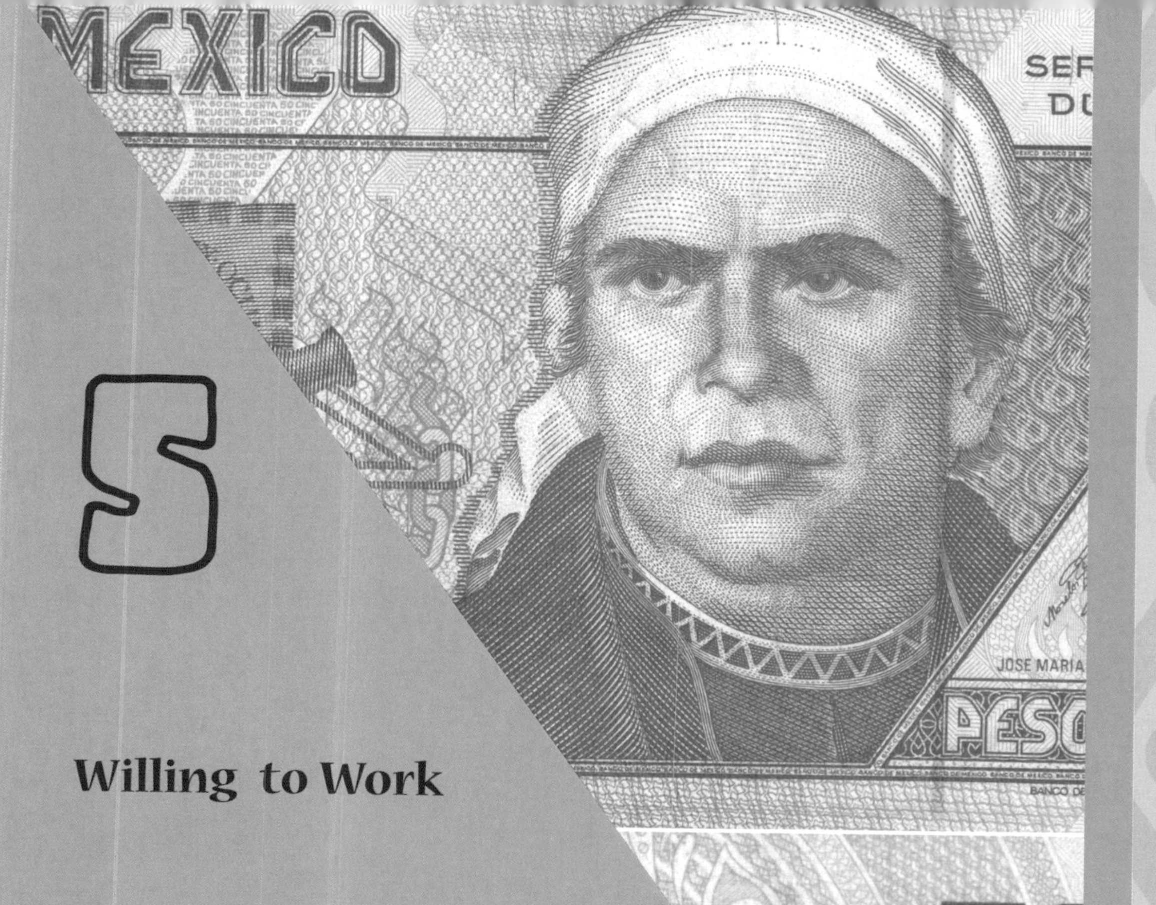

5

Willing to Work

Chuy Carbajal is sixteen and ready to head north to look for work. Like his older brothers before him, he plans to leave his tiny rural community in Jalisco, Mexico, and sneak across the border into the United States where jobs are more plentiful.

"You don't have to leave," his mother begs him. "Things are different now than they were when your brothers left. There are jobs here now. Stay with us."

The changes Chuy's mother points at came about as a result of the North American Free Trade Agreement (NAFTA). "With NAFTA we will export goods, not people," Carlos Salinas de Gortari said when he was Mexico's president. Only half of the President's promise has come true.

Young men like these often head to the other side of the border.

exports: goods sent out of the country for sale and use.

rite of passage: an event that marks a significant transition in life.

NAFTA brought American businesses across the border into Mexico. They built factories, and the factories needed workers. ***Exports*** have increased 500 percent in the Mexican state of Jalisco, and that state now ranks second in Mexico in generating jobs. But young people like Chuy are still leaving to work in the United States. Even though there are more jobs in Jalisco than there were before NAFTA, wages in the United States remain about eight times higher than in Mexico.

Tradition and culture also drive young men north. For someone like Chuy, the journey north is a ***rite of passage***, a sign that he too, like his brothers, is a man. He is following the patterns he learned from his grandfather, his father and his uncles, and his older brothers.

NAFTA

The North American Free Trade Agreement (NAFTA) went into effect on January 1, 1994; it is an attempt to establish a tariff-free trade area and to remove barriers to investment between the United States, Canada, and Mexico.

Proponents of NAFTA claim that it will lead to more high-wage jobs in the United States and an equalization between the economies of the member countries. Not everyone sees it that way. Some U.S. critics claim that the lifting of investment and trade restrictions will send businesses (and their jobs) to the other members, primarily to Mexico. Because the wages are so low there, the business owners would see increasing profit margins while American employees would be without a job. As can be expected, many business owners are in favor of the agreement, while many American labor unions are not.

Human rights activists are also concerned about the effects of NAFTA, since big businesses may exploit workers in countries where there are fewer laws to protect workers and the environment. As the world's economy becomes more and more global, many people feel we also need global laws to protect the world's workers from unscrupulous corporations.

Mexican Wages

Minus benefits, take-home pay in Mexico averages $5 per day. That's a little less than the U.S. minimum hourly wage.

Mexico's President Vicente Fox has vowed to stop the labor outflow by creating better-paying jobs at home. But that's not easy. NAFTA may bring jobs to Mexico, but American businesses are often looking to cut costs in their Mexican factories. Labor regulations and environmental laws in the United States cost factories millions of dollars; Mexico lacks these restrictions, which saves businesses money. These businesses are unwilling to lose the advantages that NAFTA has given them. As a result, the factories they build in Mexico are often unsafe, wages are low, and even children are sometimes allowed to work long hours.

"So long as a worker in Mexico earns $5 per day and a worker in the United States earns $60, immigration problems will continue," President Fox said soon after he was elected. Young people like Chuy will continue to head north across the border. If they are caught and sent back, they will try again. After all, they are strong and eager to work. It doesn't look like one the greatest global migrations of modern times will end any time soon.

A History of Migration

The flow of immigrants looking for work across the border is not a new phenomenon. Today's numbers may be higher than ever before, but for the past century, Mexican Americans have been a major part of the American workforce.

During the World Wars, the American government's *Bracero* Program brought thousands of Mexicans into the United States as temporary workers to replace the American employees who

More Effects of NAFTA

The onion fields in Mexicali are filled with babies. Toddlers wander up and down the rows, clutching baby bottles and half-chewed onions in their small, grimy fists. Younger babies sleep in blankets spread on the dirt; some are snuggled in vegetable bins where at least they don't risk being stepped on.

The babies' parents are hard at work in the fields. So are their older brothers and sisters. As many as a quarter of the workers are somewhere between six and sixteen years old. The California-based farming corporation that owns these fields employs entire families, children and all.

These children are more victims of NAFTA, the trade agreement that sent many U.S. growers across the border into Mexico. The American companies are looking to cut their costs, and the Mexican government subsidizes their efforts. As the incomes of poor Mexicans dropped by almost half, families became desperate. Thousands of children now grow and harvest the crops destined for tables in America's cities.

Mexico's constitution outlaws child labor—and yet Mexico's Labor and Social Forecasting Secretariat estimates that various economic sectors employ a total of 800,000 workers under age fourteen. Based on the 1990 census, the Public Education Secretariat estimates that more than 2.5 million kids between six and fourteen don't attend school. The long-range effects of this may cause a snowball effect that leads to deeper poverty and greater desperation. No wonder so many Mexicans want to move to the United States, whether legally or illegally.

Mexican carrot pickers in California

had gone to war. However, these workers were not authorized to stay in the country, and many were mistreated and paid extremely low wages.

Despite this, many of the Braceros did not return to Mexico. The U.S. and Mexican governments realized that the "temporary" admission of workers into the United States had not worked out the way it was intended. Many farmers became dependent on the inexpensive migrant workers and stopped trying to fill positions on their farms with more expensive local workers—and despite the low pay, workers and their families became dependent on the income provided by the farmers. Their wages were often so low, however, that some people compared the program to government-approved slavery. Faced with such problems, the program was ended in 1964.

But the flood of workers from Mexico did not ebb. Between 1945 and 1955, some 7.5 million acres of new farmland had gone into production in America's western states—and the landowners needed workers. Smuggling undocumented workers into the United States became a lucrative business.

Coyotes

People who make their living smuggling Mexicans into the United States are called coyotes. Many of these individuals have organized systems that may include fleets of trucks or buses, secret hideouts, counterfeit documents for the workers, and guides that lead illegal Mexicans across the border through treacherous rural terrain. Some coyotes are unscrupulous, and busloads of illegal immigrants have been found dead, suffocated in crowded vehicles that lacked adequate ventilation and cooling.

Undocumented Aliens

No one knows exactly how many undocumented aliens are in the United States. During the 1990s, experts estimated that there were probably somewhere between one and two million—and between 55 and 65 percent of those were Mexicans. They make up nearly 10 percent of America's population of Mexican descent.

From the 1950s through the 1980s, most of these illegal aliens found work as farmworkers, but today that situation has changed. Now, more and more skilled workers from Mexican cities are seeking industrial and urban jobs. Many undocumented Mexicans work in hotels, restaurants, car washes, and health-care centers.

A Single Labor Market

Despite the boundaries that exist between the United States and Mexico, their economies are tangled together. Unsnarling the situation has proved to be too difficult for either government. Businesses in the United States depend on Mexican workers who are

Workers unite in Tijuana to march in protest of their low-paying jobs.

Mexican workers look for better opportunities.

willing to take the lowest-paying jobs, positions that few Anglo-Americans will accept. Meanwhile, the journey north to seek employment has become a cultural ***institution*** for Mexicans like Chuy Carbajal.

Many American citizens resent these workers who come across the border. Americans fear that undocumented workers will take jobs away from Americans during a time when there are already not enough jobs to go around. ***Economics*** is a complicated subject, but experts tend to agree that Mexican workers actually have a positive effect on the American economy. The resentment of some Americans probably has more to do with prejudice than with actual economic hardships.

Ironically, Americans have always ***stereotyped*** Mexicans as lazy. The image of the napping Mexican in a big sombrero beneath a cactus is one that most Americans have seen. The reality is far different, for much of America's industry has been built on the energy and determination of Mexican workers.

Prejudice is a hard enemy to fight. Today, however, more and more Mexican Americans have learned to take pride in their unique accomplishments and identity.

institution: *an established law, custom, or practice.*

economics: *the study of the production, distribution, and use of goods and services.*

stereotyped: *made an oversimplified judgment about one group by another group.*

Habla Español

trabajadores (trah-bah-hah-door-ace): workers

empleo (aim-play-oh): job

6

A Name of Their Own: Chicanos

For most of Rosita Torres's life, being a Mexican American meant she didn't quite fit in with other people her age. Her skin was browner, her clothes somehow always looked a little different from everyone else's, and people thought her family spoke with a funny accent.

A busy Mexican restaurant in upstate New York

Rosita's parents owned a Mexican restaurant in a small town in upstate New York. The restaurant was successful, but her parents worked long hours to make it that way. Rosita and her brothers were expected to help out in the restaurant after school, and as she got older, Rosita felt embarrassed when she had to serve food to her classmates. They would smile and say hi, but Rosita felt as though they thought she were a servant, some sort of second-class citizen who could never completely measure up to their standards.

Rosita loved her family, and she was proud of her Mexican heritage. But sometimes she felt embarrassed as well. She didn't like herself for feeling that way—but she did.

When Rosita graduated from high school and went away to college, though, she discovered a whole new way of thinking about herself. At the campus she attended, she was no longer the only Mexican American; instead, she was one of a large group of friendly people her own age. What's more, the college offered a whole program on *Chicano* studies.

Rosita had been vaguely aware of the word *Chicano* before she went to college, but she had never connected it with herself. Now, for the first time, she realized there was a special name for people like her and her family, a name that affirmed how special and wonderful it was to be a Mexican American. As Rosita learned more about her own heritage, she learned to be proud of her cultural identity.

feminist: having to do with the belief that women and men should have equal opportunities and rights.

A New Word with Ancient Roots

Today, a Chicano usually refers to a Mexican person born in the United States. (*Chicana* is the female form of the word, which often also has ***feminist*** connotations.) Originally, the term *Chicano* was an offensive name used in Mexico to label a person of low class and poor morals, but Mexican Americans took the insult and claimed it as a word of pride.

***civil rights**: the rights that all citizens of a society are supposed to have.*

***activists**: people who act in support of a cause.*

***bilingual-bicultural**: in two languages and representing two cultures.*

It is an ancient word that evolved from the name of the long-ago Aztec people: the Mexica (pronounced "may-cheek-ah"). The word ties modern-day Mexican Americans to their oldest common roots. Claiming this name also carries the implication that the individual is neither from here (the United States) nor there (Mexico); instead, she belongs to both countries' cultures. For people like Rosita, being Chicano represents the struggle to fit into the world of America while still maintaining a sense of Mexico's rich legacy.

The word sprang out of the ***civil rights*** movements of the 1970s. Just as African Americans rose up and spoke out for justice during this time, so did many Mexican Americans. The Chicano civil rights movement not only sought social justice and equality for Mexican Americans, it also worked to reclaim their unique heritage through education and art.

Some experts believe that the Chicano Movement had been simmering under the surface since the end of the Mexican-American War in 1848, when the border was changed and hundreds of thousands of Mexicans suddenly became U.S. citizens overnight. The ancestors of many of these people had lived in the same area since before the Pilgrims landed in Plymouth—and yet the rest of the U.S. population often regarded them as aliens, people who were not as competent, not as socially acceptable, and generally unequal to Anglo-Americans. As a result, Mexican Americans have endured long years of discrimination, racism, and oppression.

Street murals in California express Chicano pride.

The Chicano Movement that culminated in the early 1970s was inspired by many heroes—community leaders, ***activists***, artists, educators, and researchers. Leaders such as Reis Lopes Tijerina, Corky González, César Chávez, and Dolores Huerta gave the Movement a voice. They called attention to the issues facing Chicanos—and they made an entire nation listen.

The Chicano Movement's Contributions

The Chicano Movement did not end in the 1960s or '70s. It continues to be a growing force that works to achieve a variety of goals.

For example, education is very important to the Movement. Some of its goals for Mexican American students include: a reduction of school dropout rates; improvement of educational achievement; development of ***bilingual-bicultural*** programs; and expan-

Vibrant Chicano art

lithography: printing process using a plate on which only the image to be printed takes up ink.

sion of higher education fellowships and support services. Those involved in the Chicano Movement also work to create Chicano-centered curricula, courses and programs in Chicano studies, and an increase in the number of Chicano teachers and administrators.

The arts also play a major role in the Movement. As cultural pride blossomed, Chicano visual arts, music, literature, dance, theater, and other forms of expression also flourished, and a full-scale Chicano Art Movement emerged during the early years of the Movement. Chicanos expressed their cultural heritage through painting, drawing, sculpture, and ***lithography***. Novels, poetry, short stories, essays, and plays flowed from the pens of contemporary Chicano writers. Chicano, Mexican American, and Hispanic cultural centers, theaters, film festivals, museums,

Corky González, Reis Lopes Tijerina, and MAYO

Reies Lopez Tijerina led the *Alianza de Pueblos Libres* (Alliance of Free Pueblos) in New Mexico, while Rodolfo "Corky" González founded the Crusade for Justice movement in Colorado. Their efforts became the nucleus of the Mexican American Youth Organization (MAYO).

The group of people that followed these leaders studied different political theories; they examined the works of black nationalists such as Stokely Carmichael, Elderidge Cleaver, and Malcolm X; they traveled into the South to talk with associates of Martin Luther King Jr. After the interviews were completed, reports were made back to the group, and MAYO came into being. The organization was dedicated to getting involved in issues of discrimination, police brutality, and labor organizing, as well as education and the treatment of Mexican American students in public schools. MAYO fostered a new pride in being Chicano.

In order to accomplish this task, young activists were recruited, including young Mexican American high school dropouts who had become disenchanted with the public school system. Others were high school students from the poorest districts. MAYO understood that you do not have to be an adult to work for social justice.

A street mural portrays Delores Huerta.

galleries, and numerous other arts and cultural organizations grew in number, becoming major cultural forces within the United States.

Latino Americans are the fastest-growing minority in the United States—and Mexican Americans make up the largest percentage of this group. In the years to come, they will play a growing role in the American cultural scene. American music, art, language, food, fashion, politics, and lifestyle will all be shaped by the rich heritage of Chicanos and other Hispanic groups. Unfortunately, prejudice against Mexican Americans still exists—but more and more kids like Rosita Torres are learning to claim the vital identity that is theirs.

César Chávez and Dolores Huerta

César Chávez was a Mexican American who grew up working on farms in California where pay was low. He wanted to improve the situation, so he started organizing farmworkers into a labor union that would demand higher pay and better working conditions from their employers. In 1962, Chávez and fellow organizer Dolores Huerta founded the National Farm Workers Association (NFWA) and later the United Farm Workers' Organizing Committee (UFWOC). Under the leadership of Chávez and Huerta, the UFWOC used nonviolent tactics such as protest marches, strikes, and boycotts to fight grape producers for better working conditions.

MEChA (an acronym for *Movimiento Estudiantil Chicano de Aztlán*—Chicano Student's Movement of Aztlán [the legendary homeland of the Aztec]) is one organization that has grown out of the Chicano Movement. It is dedicated to the promotion of Chicano history, education, and political action.

In 1999, MEChA adopted a document titled "The Philosophy of MEChA," which affirmed that "all people are potential Chicanas and Chicanos," and that "Chicano identity is not a nationality but a philosophy." MEChistas (members of MEChA) consider themselves neither Americans nor Mexicans, but descendants (either genetically or spiritually) of the Americas' Native people. MEChA's motto is "La Union Hace la Fuerza," "Unity Creates Strength."

MEChA is sometimes criticized for being a racist and separatist organization, with a primary goal of returning the states of California, Arizona, New Mexico, and Texas back to Mexico. These criticisms are based largely on the controversial language in *El Plan Espiritual de Aztlán (The Spiritual Plan of Aztlan*, one of MEChA's publications). MEChA leaders counter that these statements have been pulled out of context and misinterpreted, and that MEChA is opposed to oppression in all forms, including racism.

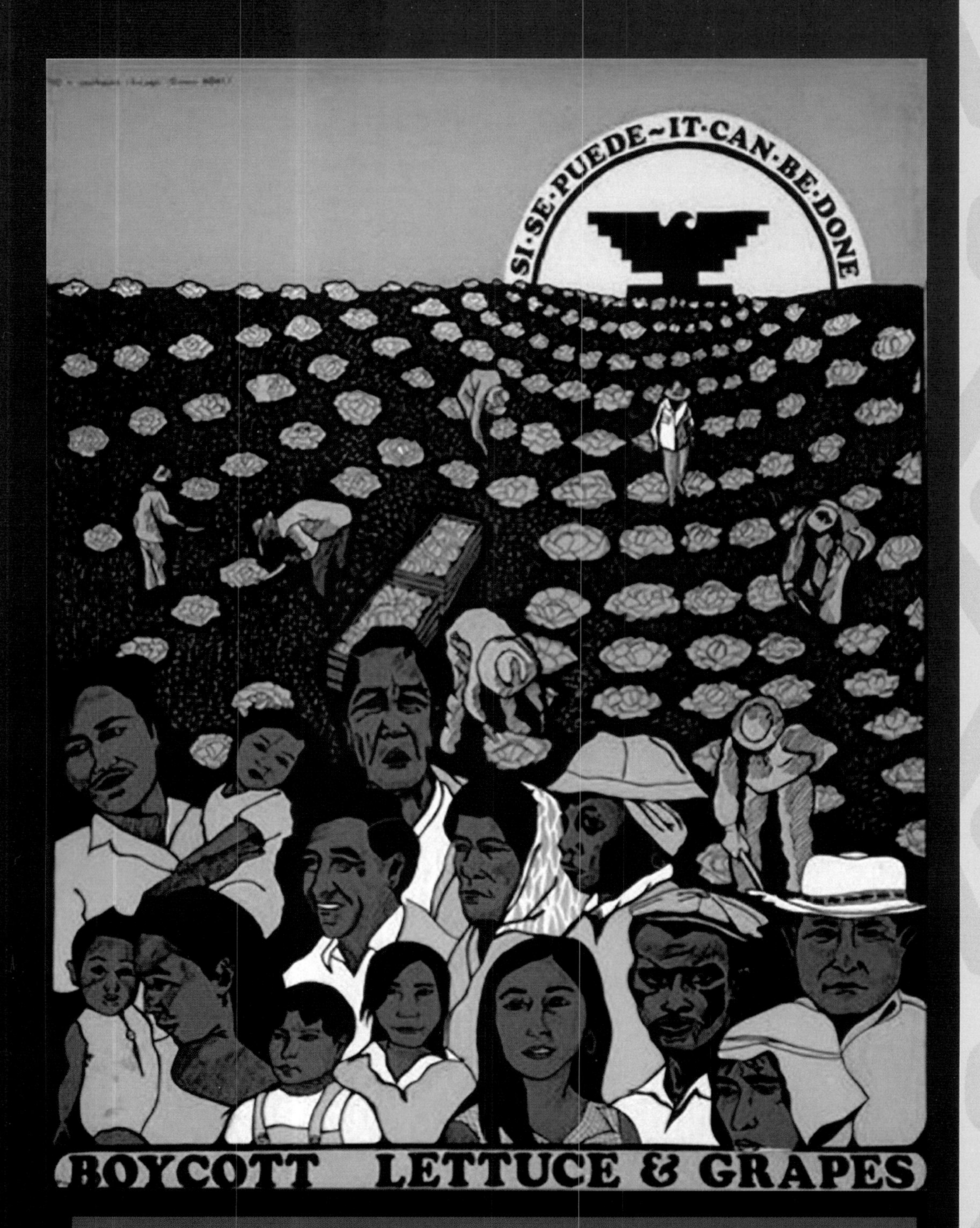

A poster calling for Americans to stop buying lettuce and grapes in support of the United Farm Workers.

Influential Mexican Americans

Entertainers

Mario López, actor
George Lopez,
actor, comedian
Jimmy Smits, actor
Paul Rodriguez, comedian
Carlos Santana, musician
Lila Downs, singer
Linda Rondstadt, singer
Selena, singer

Politicians

Cruz M. Bustamante,
Lieutenant Governor of
California
Henry Cisneros, former
Secretary of Housing and
Urban Development
Bill Richardson,
Governor of New Mexico

Sports Stars

Oscar de la Hoya,
boxing
Rudy Galindo,
figure skating
Nancy Lopez, golf
Lee Trevino, golf

Activists

César Chávez,
labor union organizer
Linda Chavez-Thompson,
labor union organizer
Dolores Huerta,
labor union organizer

Authors and Others

Sandra Cisneros, author
Rubén Salazar, author, journalist
Ellen Ochoa, astronaut
Mario Molina,
Nobel Prize–winning chemist

Mexican farmworkers

Habla Español

nombre (nome-bray): name

las artas (lahs ahr-tahs): the arts

7

Cultural Wealth vs. Economic Poverty

Fridays are taco nights in Tara Daniels' house. Tacos are an easy meal Tara's dad can make when he comes home from work, and then the whole family watches a video together. It's a good way to unwind after the busy week, and everyone likes the spicy beef, beans, and cheese; the corn tortillas; and the fresh salsa Tara's mom makes from the tomatoes she grows in the garden. Tara likes to be the one to mix the guacamole to go with the tortilla chips; she knows how to add just the right amount of lemon juice and garlic to the avocado mixture. When Tara's dad mentions that he never ate Mexican food until he was an adult, Tara can hardly believe him.

Mexican foods are American favorites.

Mexican Food, a Favorite of All Americans

In the 1840s and 1850s, when the United States gained huge pieces of what had been Mexican territory, some of the first things Americans noticed about their new neighbors were their unusual and tasty foods. By the end of the nineteenth century, Mexican foods were being incorporated into a few American cookbooks. As the years went by, many Mexican foods were adapted to appeal to American tastes—foods like chili, tortilla chips, and nachos. Over the past fifty years, Mexican American foods were commercialized, and both sit-down and fast-food Mexican restaurants have spread across the United States. Today, Mexican American foods add rich diversity to American cuisine. Their exploding popularity can be explained by both their convenience and their taste. Tortillas are almost as popular as white bread—and salsa outsells ketchup!

Carlos Santana

As a child, Carlos Santana played folk songs on the streets of Tijuana, hoping passersby would throw him some change. Today, he is one of the longest-performing and most successful rock musicians.

Carlos Santana first entered the music scene in 1966, when he formed his namesake group Santana. Their music combined Latin influences, like salsa and samba, with blues and traditional hardcore rock 'n' roll rhythms. Since his first early hits nearly forty years ago, Santana has teamed up with various artists, fusing his trademark guitar sound with jazz, blues, Tex-Mex, and other types of music. His music continues to reflect his Mexican roots, even while it explores new styles and techniques. Santana's commitment to his music, his heritage, and his spiritual values has made him respected by both fellow musicians and the public.

When Jason Webster comes home from school, he likes to go in his room, turn on his CD player, and crank the music up loud while he unwinds after his

A Los Angeles street mural portrays the Chicano heritage.

day at school. He enjoys all kinds of rock music, but lately, he's discovered Carlos Santana. Jason's mom says Santana has been around since she was a kid, but for such an old guy, Santana is pretty awesome. Jason's favorite album is *Supernatural*, especially the song "Smooth," Santana's radical collaboration with alternative-rock star Rob Thomas from Matchbox Twenty. Jason read a quote from Carlos Santana that said, "Some songs are like tattoos for your brain . . . you hear them and they're affixed to you." That's the way Jason feels after listening to Santana's music: as though his brain has been tattooed with a million brilliant colors.

Stephanie Bryant likes to take the long way when she walks home from school. The shortest route would take her down a nondescript Los Angeles street and then around the corner to her apartment building—but the longer route takes her past her favorite street mural. The bright curling colors always get her mind off whatever new

A street mural expresses the exuberance and humor of Day of the Dead celebrations.

Chicano Street Murals

During the early Chicano Movement, Mexican American artists began painting street murals that expressed their viewpoints. Murals helped spread information to both the literate and the illiterate. They became visual stories that proclaimed unity and spoke out for justice. Because of their accessibility, murals became popular in poor communities. They helped build cultural pride and empowered communities.

catastrophe has happened in her life. Each time she walks by, she notices something new: a moon with a detailed woman's face, tiny people entwined among the branches of a tree, hummingbirds sprinkled among the stars. She can't explain how the painting makes her feel; the closest she can come is the word "hopeful," as though life is full of some sort of meaning after all.

When she gets home, she takes her markers and draws her own bright images, allowing her thoughts and feelings to flow out of her in swirls of color. She can't imagine what it would be like to have the entire side of a building to cover with images.

Josh Hepler's family has started a new family tradition: a Day of the Dead celebration. Josh's mom learned about it from the Latino church she's started attending; she was so impressed that she wanted her own family to participate, even though there's not one Mexican on their family tree.

At first, Josh thought it was pretty weird and kind of silly. He didn't want anyone at school to know, so he made sure none of his friends dropped over to his house while it was decorated with candles and grinning skeletons. If any of his friends did come by, he planned to let them think his mother had decorated for Halloween in a big way this year and just hadn't gotten around to taking down the decorations. Anyway, that's what Day of the Dead seemed like—Halloween without the trick-or-treating and costumes.

But afterward, Josh had to admit he'd kind of enjoyed it. A lot of people in his family had died over the last few years—his grandpa from a heart attack, his little sister from leukemia, his aunt from breast cancer—and the Day of the Dead rituals made him feel like all the people he loved were still close by, even though they had died.

Turned out, Day of the Dead wasn't creepy and spooky like Halloween. Instead, it was a lot of fun, a time to laugh and remember and feel close to the family members who were no longer with them. Somehow, it made him feel better, as though he didn't need to be so sad and scared of death after all.

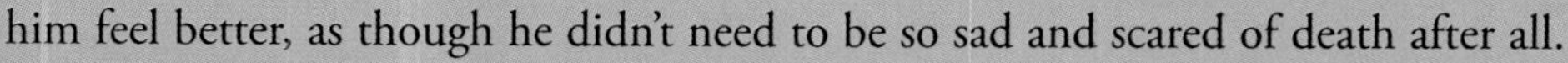

The Day of the Dead

Long ago, the Natives of Mexico believed that once a year the souls of the deceased were allowed to return from the world of the dead. During that special time, they could keep company with their loved ones and enjoy again the ordinary pleasures found in the world of the living. To guide the dead souls, their loved ones lit fires. They also strewed the way with marigold blossoms, blooms that would catch the eye with their brightness and tickle the nose with their pungent scent, reminding the dead of the earth where they once lived. People placed bowls of water for thirsty souls, parched after their journey from the other world, and they spread out the dead's favorite foods for their enjoyment. The month-long celebration was a time of laughter and feasting. Skulls smiled down on festivities from their places of honor; for these long-ago people, the skull was a symbol of hope.

When the Spanish arrived in the land that would be modern-day Mexico, the people there had been celebrating this ancient tradition for more than three thousand years. The Spanish took death very seriously, and they tried to destroy the practice.

But the Native people would not let go of either their belief or their practice. Finally, the Spanish allowed them to continue their celebrations, but the Catholic priests moved the tradition from the summer to November 2, All Soul's Day, the day set aside by the Church for remembering the dead. The Day of the Dead then evolved into a holiday practiced throughout Mexico. For many Mexican Americans today, the celebration is a statement of faith in the spiritual world's reality.

A Day of the Dead altar

Mexican pottery

Lisa Dellapenna loves going to her best friend Gloria's house. It seems like the Romeros are always laughing and hugging and telling long stories. In a way, it reminds Lisa of Christmas, when she visits her Italian grandma—except the Romeros live just down the street, instead of the other side of the country.

Gloria's house is full of beautiful things: painted pots crowd the windowsills; bright paper mobiles of birds and boats and stars dangle from the ceiling; woven rugs hang from the walls; and funny clay animals perch in odd nooks and corners. When Lisa comes in the house, she always sucks in a deep breath; the food Mrs. Romero cooks smells wonderful, and Lisa can't believe how lucky Gloria is to have Mexican food every day.

Lisa loves Gloria's family, too. Mr. and Mrs. Romero are like second parents to Lisa, and Gloria's little brothers are sweet and silly; Lisa loves chasing them around and tickling them. But Lisa's favorites are Gloria's grandparents, who live in their own little apartment upstairs. Lisa could listen for hours to the stories they tell and the songs they sing. She's glad she's learning Spanish at school, so she can understand them better. She can't imagine what life would be like without Gloria and her family.

Cultural Wealth

Most of us probably take for granted all the Mexican flavors that are part of our world today. Although we may not always notice, Mexican Americans are adding depth and color to many levels of American life—from sports to politics, religion to the arts, food to entertainment. Tara, Jason, Stephanie, Josh, and Lisa are all Anglo-Americans whose lives are being enriched by Mexican Americans and their culture.

The Chicano Movement has helped Mexican Americans value their own culture and recognize all they have to offer. But they still have a long way to go. Poverty and discrimination are all too common factors in many Mexican Americans' lives.

Economic Poverty

At the end of the twentieth century, the U.S. Census Bureau reported that the average annual family income for Hispanics in general was $29,311, about $13,500 less than the average for the entire American population. The statistics relating specifically to Mexican Americans were even worse: more than a quarter lived below the poverty line. Their unemployment rate was more than 10 percent. While 85 percent of the general population had medical insurance, only 20 percent of Mexican Americans did.

These statistics are the result of many factors, including prejudice and lack of educational opportunities. Some researchers also point to aspects of the Mexican culture that

capitalistic: *relating to capitalism, an economic system characterized by the private or corporate ownership of the means of production.*

A Mexican American celebrates his heritage with a traditional Native costume.

play a role in holding back Mexican Americans when they try to succeed. Basic cultural differences may place Mexican Americans at a disadvantage.

For example, many Mexican Americans do not place the same value on education that other cultural groups do. Hard manual labor is often valued, while reading is considered to be a waste of time. A well-educated child is considered to be a well-behaved child, rather than one who excels at learning new things.

Even Mexican Americans' deep devotion to their religion may be a factor in their lack of economic success. In America's ***capitalistic*** system, competitiveness, individuality, and assertiveness are often qualities necessary for success; it's every person for herself, and the one who pushes the hardest is the one who wins. Mexican Americans, however, often take Christian teachings very seriously; they try to practice humility, respect, and honesty. Doing your duty well, without complaint, is more important than "getting ahead," and the well-being of the entire community is stressed rather than the individual's perspective. What's more, material wealth is not valued as much as spiritual riches.

As more and more Mexican Americans take their place in American society, however, they will inevitably have greater influence on American culture as a whole. Hopefully, Mexican Americans will have increased opportunities to take advantage of all America has to offer. At the same time, the rest of America has much to learn from Mexican Americans.

In the twenty-first century, Mexican Americans need to find their place in the American worlds of education, employment, and politics. As they do so, their presence will continue to enrich and strengthen the United States.

A Los Angeles street mural expresses America's rich immigrant heritage.

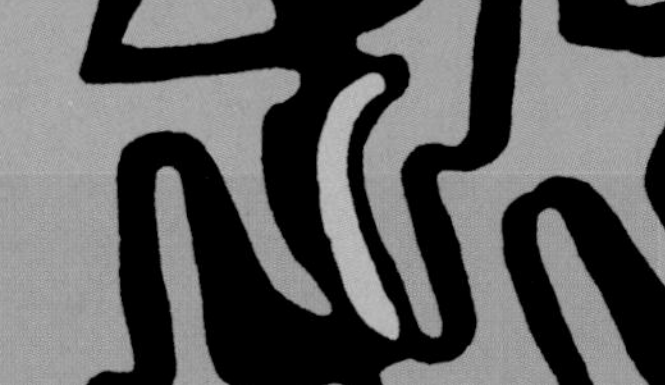

Habla Español

Día de Los Muertos (dee-ah day loce mware-toes): Day of the Dead

fe (fay): faith

Timeline

2000 B.C.–400 B.C.—The Olmecs thrive in Mexico.

1200–1500—The Mexica people form a large empire.

1325—The Mexica establish their capital at Tenochtitlan.

1469—Princess Isabella and Prince Ferdinand marry, becoming the "Catholic Royalty."

1474–1834—The Spanish Inquisition takes place.

1517—Martin Luther issues the writings that inspire the Protestant Reformation.

1523–1524—The first Catholic missionaries arrive in Mexico.

December 1531—The Virgin of Guadalupe appears to Juan Diego outside of Mexico City.

1598—The first Spanish capital is established in what is now New Mexico, beginning the Spanish colonization of the American Southwest.

September 15, 1810, 11:00 PM.—Father Hidalgo spurs citizens to action in Mexico's fight for independence with his "Grito Delores."

1814—The Mexican constitution is issued.

September 21, 1821—Mexico gains its independence from Spain.

1836—The Velasco Agreement is reached, giving northern Mexico its freedom.

February 2, 1948—The Treaty of Guadalupe Hidalgo is signed, ending the Mexican-American War.

September 19, 1985—A large earthquake rocks Mexico City.

January 1, 1994—The North American Free Trade Agreement (NAFTA) goes into effect.

Further Reading

Gonzales, Manuel G. *Mexicanos: A History of Mexicans in the United States.* Indianapolis: Indiana University Press, 2000.

Hellman, Judith Adler. *Mexican Lives.* New York: The New Press, 1994.

Hernandez, Roger E. and Amy N. Hunter, *History of Mexico.* Philadelphia, Pa.: Mason Crest, 2002.

Jovinelly, Joann and Jason Netelkos. *Crafts and Culture of the Aztecs.* New York: Rosen Publishing Group, 2003.

MacDonald, Fiona. *How Would You Survive as an Aztec?* New York: Scholastic Library Publishing, 1997.

McIntosh, Kenneth. *Latinos Today: Facts and Figures.* Philadelphia, Pa.: Mason Crest, 2005.

———. *The Latino Religious Experience: People of Faith and Vision.* Philadelphia, Pa.: Mason Crest, 2005.

Meier, Matt S. and Feliciano Ribera. *Mexican Americans/American Mexicans: From Conquistadors to Chicanos.* New York: Farrar, Straus and Giroux, 1999.

Sanna, Ellyn. *Latino Folklore and Culture: Stories of Family, Traditions of Pride.* Philadelphia, Pa.: Mason Crest, 2005.

———. *Mexican American, American Regional Cooking Library.* Philadelphia, Pa.: Mason Crest, 2004.

Stokes, Erica M. and Roger E. Hernandez. *Economy of Mexico.* Philadelphia, Pa.: Mason Crest, 2002.

For More Information

FAS online

www.fas.usda.gov/info/factsheets/NAFTA.html

Mexican Embassy

www.mexican-embassy.dk

Mexican independence

www.tamu.edu/ccbn/dewitt/mexicanrev.htm

Mexico Connect Time Line Overview

www.mexconnect.com/mex_/history.html

Mexico for Kids

www.elbalero.gob.mx/index_kids.html

MEXonline

www.mexonline.com/cultart.htm

National Latino Children's Agenda

www.nlci.org/org/About%20agenda.htm

Office of NAFTA and Inter-American Affairs

www.mac.doc.gov/nafta

Publisher's note:
The Web sites listed on this page were active at the time of publication. The publisher is not responsible for Web sites that have changed their addresses or discontinued operation since the date of publication. The publisher will review and update the Web site list upon each reprint.

Index

Picture Credits

Benjamin Stewart: pp. 9, 10, 13, 15, 16, 18, 19, 20, 24, 39, 40, 52 (top), 53, 59, 64, 68, 75, 76, 79, 80, 94, 102

Corel: p. 104

Dianne Hodack: p. 6

Library of Congress: pp. 23, 72, 89

Michelle Bouch: pp. 34, 54, 66, 78, 92

Museum of Spanish Colonial History, Santa Fe, N.M.: 52 (bottom)

PhotoDisc: pp. 26, 27, 28, 35

Photos.com: pp. 46, 63, 101

Posadas: pp. 93, 98

Tijuana Cultural Center: pp. 55, 60

To the best knowledge of the publisher, all other images are in the public domain. If any image has been inadvertently uncredited, please notify Harding House Publishing Service, Inc. Vestal, New York 13850, so that rectification can be made for future printings.

Biographies

Ellyn Sanna is the author of many nonfiction and fiction books, for both children and adults. She has traveled in the area in and around Mexico City, and she spent most of a year living and working in an orphanage in Tijuana, Mexico. Mexicans and Mexican Americans have contributed much to her life, for which she feels a debt of gratitude.

Dr. José E. Limón is professor of Mexican-American Studies at the University of Texas at Austin where he has taught for twenty-five years. He has authored over forty articles and three books on Latino cultural studies and history. He lectures widely to academic audiences, civic groups, and K–12 educators.